somewhere between the glacier
and the door.
Child, here are two hands.

COMING HOME
poems
by Lynn Shoemaker

An Ithaca House Book

I would like to thank Howard Baker, Joseph Hansen, John Harris, James Bertolino, A.R. Ammons, Robert Morgan, John Latta, Greacian Goeke, Baxter Hathaway, David McAleavey, and Eddy Garson for their help and encouragement.

Many of these poems have appeared in *Chelsea, Epoch, Abraxas, Measure, Gegenschein Quarterly, Beyond Baroque, Wormwood, Stone Cloud, South Dakota Review, Solstice, Road Apple Review, Charas, Choice, Contraband, Rainy Day, Ironwood, Granite,* and *Field.* Grateful acknowledgement is made to the editors for permission to reprint.

Cover Design by Dennis Schmidt.
Photograph by Eddy Garson.

ITHACA HOUSE, 108 NORTH PLAIN ST.
ITHACA, NEW YORK 14850

for Gretchen, Chris, and Erica

I

COMING HOME

My mother sees a face in every lightbulb.
I say bullets.
I say snow and Arctic
waves
pounding at our door.
She won't believe me. She sees
a face, her own face.
Smiling.
Her hands reach up.
Ah, the chalkwhite mime
to arrange her own shadows.

My father is gone.
His olive bag
and marching off to Greenland
during the war—
I couldn't follow him.
No Nazis invaded the island.
No shots fired. He lived
in the snow.
His hands were not strong enough.
Only his letters
came home.

A child
wandering like a shadow
a shimmering
somewhere between the glacier
and the door.
Child, here are two hands.

II

FIRST SAY

odd now
that you should be the
first to say it
so directly
out of the blue
what I had kept
unsaid
circling within me
for so long

I had thought
in a roundabout but
superior way
by my having the first say to
touch you with my
bewilderment

even now
after you are through I
feel it's slightly
unnatural this
risk of a straight reply

REMEMBER TOM JONES

"Let's take a bath," you say.
Warm water. Your nipples rise to the bubbles.
Make us a sandwich that grins,
dark bread and salami.
Cider runs down our chins like laughter.
Crazy-bones, you poke my thirteenth rib.
For fun.
For furrowing.
"Spelunker," I say, "let's find a hair
to hang by
explore the earth
together."

ANTHROPOLOGY

on my desk
House Made of Dawn   pens
pencils
ten letters   a painting
miniature of the Missouri River Bridge
near Yankton South Dakota
The Man Who Killed the Deer
my sun glasses   a jar
full of marbles
sixty-three unpublished poems
desklamp and calendar
a bell   *The Far
Field*

my wife is sleeping
my child is sleeping
a whole life laid out on their breath
in my guts a tightness
I reach out
pick up a small brass paperweight
figure of a man
he is smiling
he is holding a fish
in his arms

OUR FAVORITE FLOWER IS THE DANDELION

Each day begins with an itch,
Sunny Dog and his armies raising a chain
of islands about our ankles.
Later we worry about the goat grazing in the hall,
pheasants under the refrigerator, the dust
slowly building up on the floor.
At dusk we come together timid and curious
as deer. Polynesians
gathered on the sand looking towards our next home.
We can see the stars floating away without us.
The earthworms loosen the soil, making a place
for our flesh.

THE MARRIAGES

They sniff through their own images.
"Snow," they say, "we can't get
through the snow."
I follow their hoofprints
for any sign
of grass
leaves
new roots in the earth.
They approach me as if I
were a thicket.
"I have nothing to give," I say.
They leave their trails across my face,
in my hands.
Their breath lies at my feet
like a rug.

HUNTING OUR MARRIAGE DOWN

We've followed its wounds for so long.
Afraid of weapons. Hungry.
There is no way to turn back.
We imagine eyes
staring
mocking us from back of that tree
bush
from down under the snow.
We circle in.
It tries to shrug off fear
but fails.
Only after our tongues go mad
can we cut its throat
cut out the heart
guts.
We ask forgiveness for taking
its life.
The hide will keep our child warm
the flesh cut in halves
keep us going
separate
miles on the earth.

LOOKING AT THE INNER EYE

Like the roots of a tree
sprawled
face down in a river
vessels on the inside of the lid.
Flashes of color
root-endings left in the earth.
Pupil a snag where
the river twists around the trunk
distorted
but keeping to its course.
It is a winter tree.
No leaves to touch the rods or cones.
The brain the inner eye
a hole where the currents change
and the hundred-year-old
sturgeon
escape the ice.

THE ICICLES

Lined up like an old
farm family having their picture taken.
It's been a lean year.
The melting snow pulls them into finer and finer
points
yet they cling to the eaves
the tired roof of their house.
They feel embarrassed in front of the camera.
All they have to show are their rough knuckles
and the transparencies
between.

OLD MAN

she worries about his hearing
the church bells are so far away
and his memory
he can't find work anymore
the young man upstairs cuts the grass
seventy-five years old
his silences are the dead limbs
of a tree
every morning
she looks on as he
climbs up to cut them off

WORK BOOTS

Soft at the top. The tongue furrowed,
worn. Lower down shoe-leather
fissures, breaks into deltas,
swamps. Stem
and leaf dissolving. Giving themselves
to the soil.
The whole process stirred by our walking.
The heat of hides.
Pull them on. They are all we have
to wear.

ALMANAC

Plant from the middle, the earth's
navel,
spiraling out towards the edge
of your field. Remember
the slope
contours of the land.
Feel them out on foot before
plowing. You may stop to rest,
claiming the shade as your own.
But not the tree's roots.
Learn when the plants appreciate
your presence. Harvest
back toward the center.
There, if you watch closely,
the dead roots and stalks,
turned under, will show you
how to begin again
next spring.

FINAL DIRECTIONS

when I die
make sure I'm good
and stiff
tie three feathers around my neck
then plant me   waist-deep   head-up
on a little rise   just above
your field

I will do more for you
than scare off
crows

THE QUILT

It colors my sleep.
Threads. Twigs and buds of design.
My dreams stick their faces out.
I can hide. I can feel the needle, squeeze
and slow
pulling of past fingers. They reach
down into me field
forest of roots. Open. New-plowed.
My life comes together.
Each breath is sewn to the next.

GALAPAGOS

Darwin landed here.
Searched the shoulders for insects,
thistle-seed.
Found turtles as big as an ox.
Shells, vertebrae shaped like ploughshares.
Their trails. Their eggs laid
in the sand.
The spine from under the earth,
plowing.

ZION

near the roadside clumps of white flowers
we call them "Gideon's trumpets"
in her play Erica
picks her own names from the air
the canyon walls are slow to come out
wary
more timid than our child
they lift their mule-deer faces
test each wind
we learn how to stand
turning our bones to grass
waiting for them to come near

under strong sun
we learn how the Navaho
make their rugs
how the weavers find colors
browns and tans in the natural wool
blues in larkspur
yellow in rabbit brush flower
reds from a mixture of pigweed
and corns   we learn patterns
sky   lightning
Indians put earth in their rugs
strand by moving
strand

weave in mountains
master weavers   two or three
at the center of a 3
by 4 1/2 foot rug
weave in the mountain's
center

these rugs tell of the canyon
hands held high to the sun
praying so the earth's plants can live
and the river like a big bear
clawing the canyon's wrists
opening wounds
cutting petroglyph and scripture
into the veins of stone

III

DOODLE: THE MAD HATTER

A black-hatted man stands in a playground
a blank sheet of paper wrapped around his left ankle.
He unwraps the paper
and puts it under his foot.
He makes a footprint on the paper.
He puts the paper under his hand.
He makes a fingerprint
in the middle of the footprint.
A black spiky flower grows out of the fingerprint.
All the children line up behind the flower.
The first child smells the flower.
His parents fall silent.
The second child smells the flower.
Her parents fall silent.
One by one all the children smell
the black spiky flower.
All the parents fall silent.
The last child picks the flower
and puts it in the man's black hat.
He smiles and begins to walk away.
He limps.
His left leg is shorter than his right.

SIZES

My hand is five times
bigger than yours.
I let you grab hold of it.
Pull and put each
finger in your mouth.
Suck. Five nipples.
Five big sticks.

The dog whines.
Paws at the back door.
Stretches his hunger
halfway up the screen.
You watch him jump
at a moth playing
just beyond his
jaws.

The moth is twice
as big as
one of your eyes.
See. It is half
the size of
your hand.

CHRISTMAS BEADS

The bones of my left hand.
So you will always remember.
I cut them myself
sucked the marrow out like a crow.
Why do you reject them?
Look. The holes are still flecked
with red.

PACIFIERS

*— a baby's screams are the winds
of another world*

rattles
furry bears with no
mouths — better he should have
a cold shell caked
with salt
            rough
brown paper sacks
forked
            branch
of a tree
holes
openings
places for the winds
to go

LEARNING TO SPEAK

1

On contact
each red blood cell
captures thousands of molecules
of oxygen.
The blood's load of carbon dioxide
is discharged at
the same time
back into the lungs.
The sound ''da'' is made by
dropping the tip of the tongue
from the top suddenly
to the bottom of
the mouth and
expelling a short burst
of air.

2

to whisper
to blow sound to seed
you have learned to stay close
to candles
how to watch them speak
copy the words of
candleflame
and smoke

da-da-da-da-da

I am the blue-white
child's cry
                rocking

horse fish
father
at the center
of fire

call my name
call

IV

DRIVING WEST ON THE OHIO TURNPIKE

A late spring
confusing the trees.
The car stood in the garage five days
a blackened kernel of wheat refusing to yield its secret.

Finally the roads sprout into Ohio
California in less than a week.
My wife is driving.   I'm on the passenger
side counting fields reading *The Branch
Will Not Break*.
Each poem opens like a blessing
alone
        without a mate
the overpass at the end of each mile.
Its shadow is a hungry crow.
I'm driving through.
I don't know if it will let me go.

NIGHT VISITORS

You lock your doors
bar your windows against
the wind.
But they come in.
They stand beside your sleep.
You're lying on your back
under a dream
of a woman walking across
a bridge.
They move as if in a boat.
You can't tell
whether their eyes are open
or closed.
Sometimes they sing
but you never hear them.
They come in at night
and pull the covers up
close about your neck
and touch your forehead
a step on the waters
before they leave.

COLLABORATOR

No shame in her nipples. They harden
in the cold air.
We look on her like a grove of dying trees,
thin-armed and angry.
She reaches out as if our eyes weren't empty,
could turn to seeds.
Soon, she will turn her back on us,
pick up a long breath as if it were a pair
of silk stockings,
and walk away.

THE OCCUPATION

The moon takes our hand
turns
her face away
each time we pass a
window.
Her head has been shaved.
No one stops to tell us why
or what way we
must go.

LEARNING YOUR ABC'S   OR YOU CAN NEVER CATCH A FALLING ICICLE

Someone has tipped your
world like a baby's block
over so the A is squeezed into the floor.
All your friends all
mothers and fathers have slipped off.
Their fingers, clinging to the edge, stiffen
like a lost alphabet.
You can't hold their hands strongly enough.
In spring only the chill
will be left
asking to be forgiven.
And your scream
hanging at the head of the stairs
the letter C
just out of the baby's reach.

THAT AND THIS

and that house has a weathervane
and this one a gazebo
and that house a tower
glassed in
an Indian looking out over Lake Cayuga
cherrywood banister   *Jungle
Books* taking three steps
at a time
and that one...and this...
and I am walking down this sidewalk
my face trots at my side
man's best friend
a spider crawls towards my vagina
my child throws rocks at my photograph
I am a man   I crack open walnuts
two at a time in my fist
my brain splits in half
a convulsive coon spits blood
the trees begin burning their limbs
I see them burn
the Indian in the tower sees them burn
the coon won't look
the spider won't look
they know
when I press my hand down
into the earth
five lakes will form

MAMMOTH'S MOUTH

Wide with sloped ceilings
then long and full of tongues—
the rooms keep changing shape.
Through every window I can see its hair
its tusks—one
short like an arm sheared off at the elbow.
I hear a crash. Doors
open. My breath is led off as a hostage.
It will be tied to the missing arm
and burned.

VOTIVE

Only the smoke gains sustenance.
I have only my hands to write with.
In the mornings they sweat like cold iron pipes.
I try rubbing them together.
The blood moves slowly.
Mumbler.
Like a whiskey priest in prayer.

THE TREE

losing
leaf by leaf
the tree stiffens
like a dog mad at the mouth
it howls at what it cannot
hold

SENSOR

Each finger preys upon the grass.
I feed on signs.
My shadow spreads out underneath my feet,
at the tips of my hands.
I can sense even the most hidden
movement.
Craters crawl across the earth like locusts.
Malaria bursts into bloom.
There are no soldiers here
but the forsythia breaks into flights of gold
and the clover drops its leaves
on a wounded ant
and spider.

40

CUTTING THE NEAR SIDE

The blade cuts along the river-edge.
Between the swallows
and their caves.
Both sides have something to learn.
Listen: the rain
touches each wing just
as it touches the earth.
Now step
into the shallows
this stand of wild rice
taste the blood
before
it disappears.

PEASANT CHILD NEAR VILLAVICENCIO, COLOMBIA

You stay near the house
your house of dark doors and smoke
near your mother crossing her arms
and your father
one arm cut off at the elbow.
Your eyes come forward.
The rest of you stays behind.
You're listening to our songs
almost clapping as we dance.
We have formed a circle.
We're trying to learn the ''joropo.''
Dona Mercedes motions for the aguardiente
limes and salt.
Your fragile steps come forward
over her land
and your whisper too.
But your shadow stays behind
near your father.
It stays behind in his one remaining hand
like a machete.

v

TRANSPLANTING A TRUE CLOWN'S NOSE

It is not a false nose. It may seem to be a strawberry. Or a plum. Or even a popped balloon. But it is real. It will sprout petunias and pain. Warts, battleflags, and blood. Use a hammer and saw. Use the dullest blade you can find.

Carry it in a casket. A derby hat is too big. If it should die on the way, plant it in the center ring. Under the elephant's hooves. Call Augusto the white clown. Have him play the cornet. Have Pepe, with his flopper shoes and longjohns, with real tears in his voice, call out Fru-fru, Fru-fru, Fru-fru over and over again.

It will come back to life. Sniff. Snort. It may even start a fire and put the flames out with a cannon. Put the fires out with a black umbrella. Put them out with an egg.

If the egg does not break—for this is the ultimate test—throw the nose into prison. Prepare a trial and an execution. It is a fake. An imposter. A pretender to the clown.

NANOOK OF THE NORTH

Ice-chunks behind your ear. No blood. You
didn't feel a thing. Penguins come running
through the hole. Squealing and tumbling down
the glacier. Catch them, Sgt. Preston. Don't
let them get away. Your great lead dog King
will turn them into bones. The howls of ivory.
Whale-songs. A new language. So you can
always hear them falling. Newton. Ahab.
Saint Teresa. How does it feel to be an apple
in Antarctica?

EATING YOUR WAY TOWARD MORNING

Do not take eyes as an answer. High-rock-nesters.
Hungry. Whining They attack the light. Each
quantum. Tear at its neck. Guts. As if it were a
field mouse. Pheasant. After dark, they suck their
own spines. Memorizing. Digesting each path in the
sky.

Quick. Your eyes. Use an ax. So the sun can
rise in the morning.

SENDING YOUR TONGUE TO ANOTHER COUNTRY

A sacrifice. The operation will not be easy.
Where to cut. How many roots to take. Even with
the sharpest of knives, there will be blood.

You must decide whether to dry it or send it
directly. Most prefer to send it. It will be sub-
merged in alcohol or formaldehyde. The jar cush-
ioned between beds of shredded paper. Accidents
are rare. The carriers know how to move rapidly,
gently.

When it arrives, they will place it on display.
In a cabinet. Or on a grey wooden pedestal. Usual
brass tag for identification. A great many will come
to look. The children will try to rub their cheeks
against it or to touch it with their forefingers. The
adults will be more wary. They will circle it with
smiles. An old wise one will turn to his colleague and
say, "I can feel it beginning to make sounds. I can
understand its tones perfectly." It will stare back at
them like a Siamese fetus from behind a mirror.
After a while they will become uncomfortable
and walk away.

On one of the busiest days, an old woman will
approach the pedestal. Dressed in a black coat. Car-
rying a cane. She will not speak. Today's messen-
gers are often mute. No one will know how she
passed the visitors and guards without being noticed.
Left behind, her cane will rattle to the floor like a
petrified legbone. The belljar will be empty.

THERAPY

Every morning. Opening all the hinges of my
body. Each time I lift my knee, a second scurries
down my spine and out the back way. I take a deep
breath. A whole hour flies out. Singing.

But the center-of-time stays behind. Knocking
his head against the wall like an autistic child.
Codes. Questions. "All monsters are cookie mon-
sters," I whisper. I run faster. Sometimes I think
I see his fingers relaxing. Like ropes let down from
too high a place. Or the muscles moving in his jaw.
Then he turns. Caught back by the deep cracks in
his hands.

I stop running.

Oh child, go to sleep. Do not worry that your
friends are gone.

SONG OF THE TOES

Look to your toenails. Through them you can
see your cells choosing up sides. Your very marrow
bending over its work like a shoemaker. Each drop
of blood pushing its cart from organ to organ, call-
ing out "vegetables, fresh fruit and vegetables."

Diggers and grubbers. Familiar with the soil.
Short-handled tools for mixing manure and old
cornstalks. They know nothing of the crow. The an-
cestral claw. They grow. Turn to fields to keep your
feet from slipping. Leaves. Humus. To give your
produce shelter.

Fruit spoils first. All ten toes keep time. Ten
garbage cans. Ten clankety lids. The Grouch lives
in the trash. He will conduct the choir. After the
voices, we will all be nailed down tight. Ready.
Safe for the earth.

VI

EXTERMINATING ANGEL

...the one taking care of us.
We flow in his veins.
Around in a big circle
gesturing at the slippery walls.
As if we expected our cries to be heard.
Something done in the heart.

His wings fold out.
They are soft and invisible.
They form a barrier, a barrier
of silence and an open door.
He would have us be as curling smoke
under a chandelier.
Already we forget that we are dry
and hot.

He is taking care...
Have you seen him? The exterminating angel.
To you he will give a goldfish
with a bloody tail. To me
a pomegranate. Red desert
shroud
and seeds.

THE BELLS

He humped them.
High in the church tower
tugged and hung on the bell-ropes
like an ape.
He hated the people in the streets
sluts beggars
who knew only the sound of carts.
They whipped him once.
Laughed jeered as the king's man
laid snakes across his back.
All but one.
Later he gave her sanctuary
tipped the cauldrons
counting the dead and mocking them
as the molten
wax hissed around their bodies.
He died
face full of fangs and slobber
uglier than any of them.
His hump full of blood
and ringing.

SIN EATER

In medieval times there was a folk
practice (never entirely stamped out
by the church) that the son
ate the father's sins. Apples,
cheeses, great slabs of bacon,
roast lamb, cakes dipped in butter—heaped
around the corpse. You ate,
screamed and begged God
that the sins flow into your body.
The food was good. More than you'd ever
eaten before. Soon you fell
to your knees. Caved in, howling
like a sick dog, you
prayed for a son of your own.

WHITE PHOSPHORUS

*Scientific studies reveal that it
burns as long as there is flesh.*

Grandfather son
buffalo—
their bodies glow at night
like the eyes around their villages.
The wounds howl
burn till they reach the Arctic
place of bones.
They tear at their own jowls.
Starve.

FAMILIAR

So my mother you've taken to
for your sleeping
the upright position.
Not that sitting up lacks grace.
It has the grace of a cat's be nimble
eyes just after playing cat
and mouse.
    Grace
of a feather refusing
to lie down.
Rest.

So you would always
be swinging.
Young girl full
new washed starched ironed
dress all white.
Though not very high.
Poised just beside Alice
just beyond the ten o'clock news
scattered balls of paper
all the whispers.

Poet-sons would push your swing
softly and singing
    "Lie down
lie down and open yourself
up to your dying.

A cat. A purring. Your own cat
in your own darkness.''

Not me.
Your death waits for the two of us.
Familiar in so many ways.
The electricity staring at you all night.
Stickpins lying on the floor.
The words of your last letter.
Familiar
though never written.

THE SUICIDE

she would rather have flown
if only for a second
catching at the leaves as she fell
she would've welcomed the hard
black hands at the bottom

> a neighbor-girl told me they had to
> build a new bridge
> with a high wire fence
> because so many were jumping
> off the old one
> she told how she and her friends
> had climbed up under
> the old bridge
> how a beam had broken free
> and passed
> close to her face

she would rather have flown
and if there had been enough hands
it wouldn't have mattered
they could've all
walked down the gorge
together

WILD GEESE

We are the islands
                reeds
      cold shells
shoreline and gravel runs you
left behind.
All summer you taught us how to move
what steps to leave in the water
how to clear the tops
          of trees
when to turn away, circling off to another
                lake for food.

Soon, you'll be out of reach.
Your honking settles like a dead
                          child
                into a half-
frozen marsh.
You could've learned from our listening
            the rocks resting
      between the tree roots the bottom
of the lake.
We could've taught you to
curl to a beginning
and be still.

PALLBEARER

Our breath settles.
Mist.
Your lungs folded in prayer.
I lay the old songs
beside you.

I mourn with my hands,
the tightening muscles in my shoulders.
Cars pull away from the church
like slivers
whittled from a dark piece of wood.

No one touches the flowers.
The grain knots and flows,
faults where the earth will enter.

This tree.
Roots.
You will be drawn into it
like a drop of water.

I pass under,
for a moment clutch at its bark,
then leave.

THE BURIALS

Plant them. Plant the rice too
sending respect down to the grandfathers.
Soon the old ones sit up
lifting themselves into each full
stalk.
The land invites us
to sit with the whole family
and eat.

INCENSE

You taught me to circle your house
sprinkling ashes.
I will come into you
as a man dressed in saffron.
Your breathing is a lotus.
I would lift it up
as smoke.

LETTING GO

*I've watched many people die and told
them they were going to die and that
this is the supreme opportunity for
human happiness—to let yourself go
entirely and stop caring.*

Alan Watts

The face is the last to go.
You have forgotten your hands
and your feet rest quietly on the floor.
But your cheek muscles tighten against the silence
and your jawbones horde the soft
beginnings of words.
You want to open your eyes
gather up your breathing
care for it
a seedling in your lungs.

Leaves blow across your skin
into your eyes
and throat
like hands cutting down a forest.
They clear the brush away
until only the clearing
is left.
Without a fire.
Without awakening or sleep.

HONYAK LEARNS TO RIDE

You taught me to ride. Close to the snags
twistings of the river.
"Forget the saddle. Grip
with your knees," you said, "hard
into the bones of her belly."

Each tree laid out traps.
The river too.
"Accept the moon," you said, "she will take
nothing from you. Move,
your shadow will move with you."

But the horse shied, turned
sensing a lighter load.
And part of us was gone.

> (Tomas Tomas knew when he was dying.
> He was ready.
> He led his horse up the mountainside.
> Above the snowline.
> His horse looked over him as he
> curled into the snow.)

Only our poems can make this journey,
the blessings wandering up the mountain
smiling as the flesh
loosens and the sun begins to warp
them to whiteness.

The mountain is a spotted antelope. Our shadow
its mate, feeding
on the prairie grass
and sun.

SLEEP

A great hall.
The floor is made of stone.
My feet have no place to go.
I have no feet.
The walls are like the sides of a fish.
There are no doors.
First the land comes in.
Then the sky fills the room
as red-threaded gills pulse open
and shut.
The wine cackles in the cups
like dice,
the eyes of a cockerel.
My blood tells my fortune—
"Your breathing will be carved up for supper.
It will be served last.
You will enjoy it
and ask for more."

CONTENTS

Lynn Shoemaker. I grew up in South Dakota. The
Missouri River. Farmland. I was half-ignorant and
half-afraid of both. But something from the land
followed me as I went off to Harvard, taught, wor-
ked in the movement (mainly in Los Angeles),
married, became a father, separated, wrote. Some-
thing from the land followed me. Inside. And from
the river, too.

$2.95